Managing

Resources

*YOUR SELF-
DEVELOPMENT
ACTION PLAN*

PETER GRAINGER

 NP

Kogan Page Ltd, London
Nichols Publishing Company,
New Jersey

First published in 1994

Apart from any fair dealing for the purposes of research or
private study, or criticism, as permitted under the Copyright,
Designs and Patents Act, 1988, this publication may only be
reproduced, stored or transmitted, in any form or by any means,
with the prior permission in writing of the publishers, or in the
case of reprographic reproduction in accordance with the terms of
licences issued by the Copyright Licensing Agency. Enquiries
concerning reproduction outside those terms should be sent to the
publishers at the undermentioned address:

Kogan Page Limited
120 Pentonville Road
London N1 9JN

© Peter Grainger, 1994

Published in the United States of America by Nichols Publishing,
PO Box 6036, East Brunswick, New Jersey 08816

British Library Cataloguing in Publication Data

A CIP record for this book is available from the British Library.

ISBN (UK) 0 7494 1250 X
ISBN (US) 0-89397-435-8

Typeset by the author
Printed and bound in Great Britain by Biddles Ltd, Guildford and
King's Lynn.

CONTENTS

PREFACE

It has taken more than 20 years to refine the 12 generic skills of management, which are the foundation of the Manager's Toolkit series, into a form which is both straightforward enough for busy managers to learn and which actually works in real life.

The skills contained in the original *Manager's Toolkit* manual and the linked style definitions were developed in the course of 15 years' management experience in senior training and development positions with Rank Xerox. Unique opportunities existed in the company at that time for creative approaches to the training and development of first-level and middle managers on both sides of the Atlantic.

As a member of a number of specialist teams in the USA and Europe, I was fortunate to come into personal contact with many of the most effective management techniques of recent times – for example, the systematic approach of Charles Kepner and Ben Tregoe and the Huthwaite Research Group's 'Interactive Skills'.

The first step was to build these techniques into a set of 'Management Standards' which the management teams of Rank Xerox's manufacturing plants in the UK developed over a number of years, and then test them in *practical* situations, including residential training programmes.

Every manager participating in a training programme brought a real-life problem to the course, and the skills taught were applied to each of those 'issues' during the programme. If a technique did not work or took too long to apply, it was discarded or modified.

After ten years of running intensive management development programmes at all levels, we had so refined the techniques that they could be integrated into a comprehensive 'toolkit' of skills that would actually guarantee results (pages 10–12).

At this time, my later business partner, Roger Acland, and I developed the personal style definitions which became an essential ingredient of all our work, and from which I later created the 'Personal Development Toolkit' and the Style Profile (page 37).

This integrated learning approach, built upon the need for positive thinking (page 24), has proved its special value to groups of managers and potential managers drawn from a wide range of organizations, from students, accountants, and engineers to teams in Allied Lyons, Rank Xerox and British Telecom.

The great benefit of the approach is that it is quick to use, flexible – *and it works*. After years of practical application, the 12 skills have now been honed to such simple effectiveness that they can be readily acquired through open learning. Look through the structure and methodology of the book to see how the approach works in practice for the three 'Resource' skills contained in this manual.

I believe the hundreds of organizations of all sizes that have purchased the original *Manager's Toolkit* manual since its publication in 1992 provide ample confirmation of the simple effectiveness of both the content and the method of learning.

Peter Grainger

INTRODUCTION

INTRODUCTION

1. The approach

The Manager's Toolkit series is designed to be suitable for a wide range of managers. You may already be a manager responsible for the work of other people and want to learn how to make more of yourself and the resources under your control. You may be facing the prospect of the responsibility of managing – or you may want to take an opportunity to manage when it arises – and be uncertain how to set about it.

To make the most of the books in the series you will either not have received any management training or the training you have received will have only given you *knowledge* of management and not the practical skills of *how* to manage.

Statistics show that few managers have received any formal training. I suspect most managers are too busy – or too exhausted – to find time to study 'management' literature. The style of each book in the series is therefore as economical and as visual as possible, concentrating on making clear each step of each process or skill – more like a DIY car manual than a learned business treatise.

The series will not only explain the essential generic skills of managing yourself and others but will give you opportunities to *practise* those skills as you apply them to your own real-life situations. The comprehensive Index on pages 95 and 96 provides you with easy access when you have a specific skills need.

In addition to acquiring such essential skills as specifying targets and standards and chairing meetings, you will come to understand yourself better, the person behind the manager or potential manager.

Some people master some of the skills of management more readily than others because of the sort of *person* they are. Some people are good with information but not with people, others are good with people but poor at taking action.

You will analyse your *personal style* in relation to three style definitions and as a result determine which are the most important skills for you personally to work on (see pages 38–9). You can therefore create your own development plan from the moment you buy the first book, confident that you are using your learning time most effectively.

Finally, you will gradually build up a *positive approach* to the situations in which you find yourself as a manager. Developing positive expectations of people and situations is a critical part of leadership and management. It has to be acquired and continuously worked at. It is not just a matter of attitude, but of applying particular techniques. Anyone can learn these techniques and so make a remarkable difference not only to the way they manage but also to the impact they make on the world about them.

2. The toolkit of skills

The Manager's Toolkit series consists of four personal development workbooks designed as open learning training and development aids to enable anyone who wants to be able to manage – or manage better – to acquire the necessary skills in their own time and at their own pace.

The series is based on the single volume *The Manager's Toolkit*, which I published in 1992, and was bought by large numbers of human resource specialists in large and small organizations throughout the United Kingdom. It was felt that making the *Toolkit* available *as a series* in a smaller format at lower cost would bring it within reach of individual managers and potential managers as and when they required each group of skills.

The concept of an *integrated* 'toolkit' of skills provides you with the opportunity to use the skills in sequence (for example in a major project), or skill-by-skill according to your personal need.

The formation of the toolkit shown opposite was the basis of the original *Manager's Toolkit*. The 12 key skills emerged from more complex models, and in numerical sequence represent a sequential, cyclical *process of management*, from clarifying roles (1) to giving and receiving feedback (12).

Each skill is not only important in its own right, but also links with its neighbours in making up *clusters* of skills for particular purposes, for example in this model to provide a

The Toolkit of Skills

a process of management

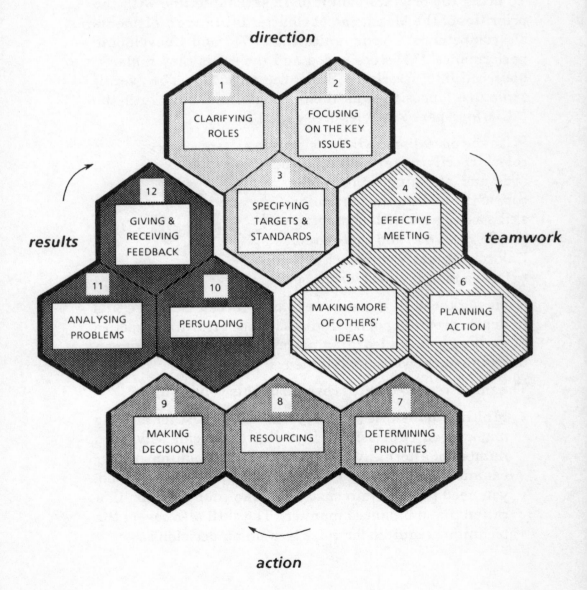

direction

1 CLARIFYING ROLES

2 FOCUSING ON THE KEY ISSUES

3 SPECIFYING TARGETS & STANDARDS

12 GIVING & RECEIVING FEEDBACK

4 EFFECTIVE MEETING

results

teamwork

11 ANALYSING PROBLEMS

10 PERSUADING

5 MAKING MORE OF OTHERS' IDEAS

6 PLANNING ACTION

9 MAKING DECISIONS

8 RESOURCING

7 DETERMINING PRIORITIES

action

sense of *direction*, to help your group to work as a *team*, to get plans turned into *action* or to make sure you actually get the *results* you set out to achieve.

To bring the original toolkit of 12 skills into line with the priorities of the Management Charter Initiative's 'elements of competence', 'communicating' (7) and 'developing performance' (11) were added and the skills they replaced absorbed into associated skills (see page 11). The overall structure (opposite) was then brought into line with the MCI's four-part 'key roles' (see page 17).

With the *operations* skills of 'clarifying roles', 'specifying targets and standards' and 'planning action' at the core of the toolkit, the particular skills associated with managing *people, resources* and *information* link conveniently with each of them to form a toolkit model for the series.

Each workbook in the series explores three essential skills in depth, providing opportunities for *open learning* practice at each step of the learning process. The process, common to all the workbooks, is explained on pages 18-19.

The three 'resource' skills covered by this volume are:

- **Making decisions** (8) is a systematic process for making major resource decisions. If you have to decide between a number of alternative pieces of expensive equipment, for example, or between a shortlist of applicants for a job, you need to be certain that you make your selection in a rational and balanced manner. The skill also covers the technique required for quick 'yes' or 'no' decisions.

The Manager's Toolkit Series

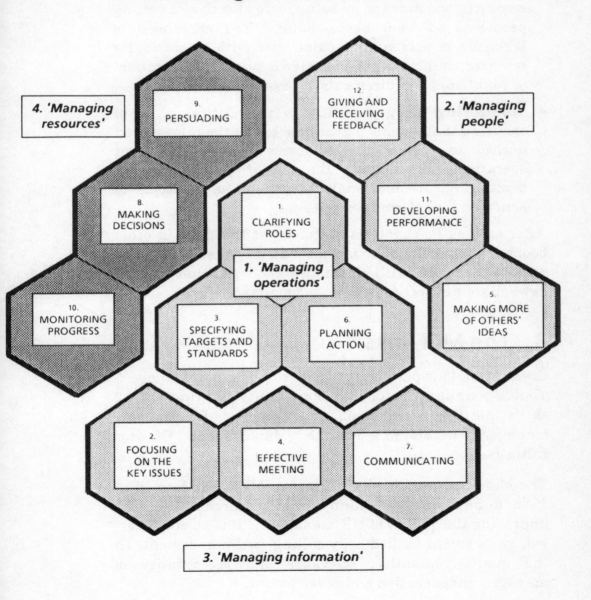

4. 'Managing resources'

9. PERSUADING

12. GIVING AND RECEIVING FEEDBACK

2. 'Managing people'

8. MAKING DECISIONS

1. CLARIFYING ROLES

11. DEVELOPING PERFORMANCE

1. 'Managing operations'

10. MONITORING PROGRESS

3. SPECIFYING TARGETS AND STANDARDS

6. PLANNING ACTION

5. MAKING MORE OF OTHERS' IDEAS

2. FOCUSING ON THE KEY ISSUES

4. EFFECTIVE MEETING

7. COMMUNICATING

3. 'Managing information'

- **Persuading** (9) enables you to make the most of the resources you manage by being more effective at getting people to do what needs doing. You may need to persuade a person to provide you with a particular resource, or include persuasion in a formal 'presentation' of your budget requirements, for example.

- **Monitoring progress** (10) is the critical skill of ensuring that you have available to you the information needed to control the resources deployed in your operation. It includes the encouragement of self-monitoring, problem analysis, and taking appropriate action on the information received.

After each skills chapter a model shows the skills in other books in the series that are most closely associated with each of the three skills in this workbook, so that you can develop your expertise in a focused manner.

3. The MCI links

Creating a four-part series from the original *Manager's Toolkit* manual provided an opportunity to bring the 12 skills into line with the national standards for first line managers developed by the Management Charter Initiative.

The Management Charter Initiative (MCI) was formed in 1988 'to improve the performance of UK organisations by improving the quality of UK managers'. It is an employer-led, government-backed body calling for improvements in the quality, quantity, relevance and accessibility of management education and development.

After extensive consultation, research and testing, the MCI is establishing a framework of four levels for management and supervisory development (Supervisory, Certificate, Diploma and Masters), with assessments based on demonstrated ability to manage. The guidelines at each of these levels give clear guidance on what is expected of managers at different levels, providing specific requirements for their development and assessment.

Detailed standards have been established for Supervisors, First Level Managers and Middle Managers, and I have taken the *First Level Management Standards* as the most appropriate link to the skills in the Manager's Toolkit series. They provide the management reference point for the National Vocational Qualifications at Level 4.

The standards first break down the key *roles* of management into first *units* and then *elements of competence*. Those covered in this workbook are:

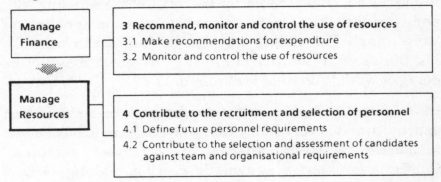

Manage Finance	**3 Recommend, monitor and control the use of resources**
	3.1 Make recommendations for expenditure
	3.2 Monitor and control the use of resources

Manage Resources	**4 Contribute to the recruitment and selection of personnel**
	4.1 Define future personnel requirements
	4.2 Contribute to the selection and assessment of candidates against team and organisational requirements

In Section 5 of Chapter 1 in this workbook (pages 39-40) you will also find links to the MCI's *Dimensions of Personal Competence*. These are included to reinforce the importance of what the MCI calls 'being personally effective' as a manager. Chapter 1 will expand this critical dimension in the context of your own *personal* development.

In this workbook, 'manage finance' has been broadened into *Managing Resources* to cover *all* resources, and includes 'making decisions', a skill essential to managing resources, and especially to 'contribute to the recruitment and selection of personnel' (*Unit 4, opposite*).

The first three elements of Unit 6 – '*plan, allocate...work*' – have been included in the 'operations' workbook because they link effectively with clarifying roles, tasks and plans.

As a result, a number of references in Element 6.4 (eg 'organizational guidelines' and 'systems/procedures') link directly with the skills in *that* workbook, rather than the skills in *Managing People*.

In this 'Resource' workbook, 'recommending... the use of resources' (3.1) is covered by the skill of 'Persuading' (9), and includes the more formal persuasion process of 'presenting'. Persuading may also be required in 'controlling the use of resources' (3.2), when a person may not be doing or want to do what is required.

In order to make recommendations on significant expenditure it is very likely that you will have to have made a choice between alternative potential resources. Confirmation that a systematic decision-making process has been employed will help to persuade the fund-holders of the validity of the request being made.

'Contributing to the recruitment and selection of personnel' (*Unit 4*) requires a clear appreciation of the criteria for selection (eg a jobholder specification) and clear adherence to those criteria during the 'selection and assessment'. Only

MCI key roles and units of competence for first line managers

Manage Operations

1 Maintain and improve service and product operations

2 Contribute to the implementation of change in services, products and systems

Manage Finance

3 Recommend, monitor and control the use of resources

Manage Resources

4 Contribute to the recruitment and selection of personnel

Manage People

5 Develop teams, individuals and self to enhance performance

6 Plan, allocate and evaluate work carried out by teams, individuals and self

7 Create, maintain and enhance effective working relationships

Manage Information

8 Seek, evaluate and organize information for action

9 Exchange information to solve problems and make decisions

Crown Copyright © 1989-1992 inclusive

a formal decision process with essential and desirable criteria can provide it, particularly when a decision is a shared responsibility.

'Monitoring and controlling' (Unit 3) link precisely with the information, analysis and action content of chapter 4, 'Monitoring progress'.

4. The method of learning

The book is laid out with explanations of each skill on the left and blank forms on the right for you to complete step-by-step in parallel with each explanation (except pages 66-69). You will find it helpful to read through *the whole* of the explanation for each chapter on the left before starting to complete the practice forms on the right, in order to see each step in its context.

In the practice forms on the right you will always be asked for information from *your own work situation*, so that the effort you put in will be repaid by consistently providing you with practical material for use on the job. At the bottom of each box on every practice sheet you will find sample answers to guide you towards your own answer.

The explanation and practice sheets for each of the three skills are followed first by a completed worksheet or questionnaire, and then by an identical blank format for you to fill in for yourself.

The *worksheet* is designed to pull together all the steps of each process and to act as a summary of the skill you have just worked through; it is also a useful reminder of the skill as you look for opportunities to practise. The *questionnaire* acts as a checklist for each skill *after* practising, and should be completed as soon as possible after the experience.

The process works like this:

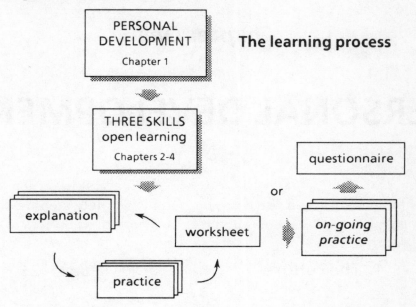

The learning process

After the open learning practice available in this book, first section-by-section, step-by-step, and then on each summary worksheet, *immediate practice* at work to secure the skills is most important. But valuable practice opportunities also exist *outside* the working environment in low risk domestic or social situations.

Buying a house, a car or even the annual holiday are major *personal* decisions which benefit from the use of the systematic process.   There are plenty of opportunities for persuasion outside work, from difficult neighbours to reluctant bank managers! Any sub-contracted work at home or delegated action from a committee will require a degree of monitoring – and even a little problem-solving.

All skills require practice to perfect and the skills of management are surely important enough for us to aim for constant improvement – if not quite perfection!

Chapter One

PERSONAL DEVELOPMENT

Chapter One

PERSONAL DEVELOPMENT

1. The culture

The climate and culture at work, created by management at all levels, is critical to acquiring key skills as part of our personal development. We may need to learn and practise certain skills relating to better control of resources but see all around us waste and inefficiency. It requires a very special type of individual to develop and maintain discipline and control in such a culture.

Control of costs and the maximization of resources are now considered all-important and a poor example from management in this area is unlikely to be a problem. Yet it may well be that in such a climate demanding constant results, short-cuts are taken, disciplines overlooked and the agreement of standards ignored. Short-termism may become the order of the day, 'fix-it-quick', 'seat-of-the-pants' management, with no investment in the resources required for *long-term* performance.

'Managing resources' requires *self-discipline*, for example to balance short-term with long-term considerations, to collect evidence before assuming the cause of a problem, and to find time to think through the factors involved in important decisions.

Too disciplined and narrow an approach to managing resources, on the other hand, can lead to staff manipulating of figures to produce the result required, or an assumption that whatever emerges from a computer must be the prime guide to determine all a manager's priorities.

Monitoring progress and managing resources means keeping in *personal* touch with the elements of performance that do not appear on computer printouts. It should increasingly mean encouraging individuals and teams to take responsibility for monitoring *their own* performance. Monitoring in this way requires not only managers with the personal touch, but also managers who are prepared to trust their staff, to allow them the freedom to manage themselves on a day-to-day basis against agreed standards.

The degree of monitoring and follow-up re-quired will depend on the degree of trust that can be placed in the individual or individuals concerned. But a manager who demonstrates his trust and high expectations of another person is rarely be disappointed.

This brings us back to that essential ingredient of management performance, *integrity*. Treating each member of your staff consistently, avoiding short-cuts or easy options for the sake of a quiet life, facing up to difficult decisions and confronting uncomfortable problems, are all required of a responsible resource manager.

It is similar with financial considerations. So often short-term financial decisions are made as a result of information received, without any thought being given to the long-term benefits that might accrue. 'Opportunity cost', or the cost of *not* doing something, playing safe and not seeing the potential benefits around the corner, can be just as damaging to the resources we manage as irresponsible risk-taking.

Again, limited vision can restrict our view of the cost of quality. Everyone is aware of the cost of quality systems and procedures, the cost of quality training, the cost of consistently meeting customer requirements etc, but how about the cost of *not* doing all of these things? Do we know the cost of complaints, the cost of putting things right, the cost of regular errors, the cost of under-used equipment etc, etc?

One of the most important elements in a culture that encourages effective resource management is *enthusiasm,* the belief that things can – and should – be done better, and the resulting ability to inspire others to make continuous improvement actually happen (see 'Drive' style on page 30). Getting the best out of the resources you manage – whether they be people, systems, machines or space – requires continuous commitment to finding new and better ways of utilizing them.

So the climate in which managers can develop their resource skills requires self-discipline, trust, imagination and enthusiasm. It is all about a *sense of responsibility* – a constant awareness that as managers we have to make the most of the resources we control. It is the challenge, but also the pleasure, of being a manager – *and it can be fun!*

The self-teach open learning method of this workbook will help you to develop three critical skills that you need to manage resources. They are not easy skills to acquire, but you will be able to develop them as and when you need them, in your own time and at your own pace. You and those you manage will then be working in an environment which is under control, with everyone and everything known to be working to their full potential.

2.   The Pygmalion Effect

The way management is performed around us creates a culture in which we feel able – or not – to develop our full potential. The right *attitude* is critical to managing ourselves and other people, and the development of a *positive* attitude is essential before setting out to acquire particular skills. Understanding the Pygmalion Effect is a helpful first step.

The essence of the Pygmalion Effect lies in the power of positive *expectations*. The word 'Pygmalion' comes not from George Bernard Shaw but from Greek mythology. Pygmalion was a sculptor in Cyprus who carved a statue of a girl which was so beautiful that he fell in love with it. So powerful were his expectations and his will that Venus stepped in and turned the statue into human form – and they both lived happily ever after!

Positive thinking has been proved to be critical to success; positive expectations of an outcome increase the likelihood of a successful result. The conscious development of positive thinking and of high expectations of ourselves and others can have a remarkable effect on our confidence, our relationships and our success.

But we can be easily influenced by the attitudes of those around us. How often have we heard the remark, 'Morale has never been lower.'? It is a phrase guaranteed to produce a self-fulfilling prophecy – the more people go around saying it, the more it becomes a reality. The attraction of thinking negatively along with everyone else – about the organization, the boss, other departments, staff, suppliers, facilities, equipment etc, etc – can prove quite irresistable!

2. The Pygmalion Effect

2.1 Write down a recent situation in which you have had a problem with a resource you manage:

Our departmental photocopier keeps breaking down at critical times

2.2 What was your attitude to this situation when you approached it, or your expectations of the resource when it happened?

'Oh, not again! The machine is rubbish - we must replace it'

What was the effect of your attitude on what happened?

I didn't ask for the cause - I just assumed the machine was faulty. We notice it more when we're very busy

2.3 If your approach was negative, how might you have been more positive towards the situation or the resource concerned?

Get it put right to deal with the crisis, and ask for analysis of causes of recent break-downs from Jane

To manage our resources effectively we have consciously and continuously to ensure that we are not drawn into adopting negative expectations of people – or things. We need to make a specific and conscious effort to identify the positive elements in any resource in order to retain an essential *balance*. 'Could the glass be considered half-full as well as half-empty?' *It is surprising how easy it is to think of the positive factors in a performance if we just stop to consider for a moment.*

While inanimate resources are of course not themselves affected by negative expectations, the *perception* of their performance is. The feedback – or public perception – that circulates about how well a particular system, machine or material is performing can be easily affected by 'negative Pygmalion'. One instance of poor performance can quickly develop into minor hysteria, if evidence is not collected and studied through a process of genuinely unbiased monitoring.

So as resource managers it is critical to have methods of monitoring in place to provide you with *reliable information* on performance so that you are not unduly influenced by the infectious power of negative feedback. The bandwagon of collective grumbling can prove highly seductive!

In the end our *confidence* affects whether we manage situations positively or negatively. We require confidence in ourselves in order to have a positive influence on other people and their attitudes. To have that confidence we need to *understand ourselves*, to be aware of our natural strengths and to recognize our limitations. The next section will enable you to do just that.

2.4 Write down a situation in the future in which you believe you will have to deal with a resource problem :	*Proposal from Jim to replace our 'unreliable' copier for discussion at next team meeting*
2.5 What are your expectations of that situation?	*The machine does seem to let us down at critical times; staff fed up with it*
If your expectations are negative, how is it likely to affect the outcome?	*We won't have a balanced discussion based on the evidence in Jane's report*
2.6 Think of the positive factors involved and how you could use them to make your expectations more positive :	*Jane's report suggests staff aren't operating machine properly, and performance not abnormal - we just notice them more at crisis times*

3.   Personal style

Our ability to manage some situations and not others, to manage some people and not others, is partly a question of the sort of person we are, our personal style. If we understood more about our style it would help us to know and to develop our natural strengths and to accept or overcome our limitations.

The three styles we developed are very simple and represent the basis of 'what makes people tick'. They first emerged as a result of considering an interesting model of motivation, which exactly reflected the result of the research we were doing at the time into leadership styles and the means of identifying *potential* managers.

HEAD
+
HEART
+
FEET
=
MOTIVATION

The first distinct style is **'Analyse'** (or 'Head') to represent the thinking, analytical type of person; the second is **'Bond'** (or 'Heart'), the feeling, caring type of person; the third is **'Command'** (or 'Feet'), the active, results-orientated type of person.

Each style can be summed up as follows:

'ANALYSE' (or 'Head')
Values logic and distrusts subjective judgements; able to provide considered and rational arguments; keen to see rules and procedures applied.

'BOND' (or 'Heart')
Conscious of the importance of mutual understanding and stresses the benefits of working with people; seeks to get the best out of others by trust and encouragement.

'COMMAND' (or 'Feet')

Likes to be in control of people and events, quickly responding to job demands and opportunities; trusts own judgement and acts on conclusions; inclined to use incentives and sanctions to influence results.

A high-scoring 'Analyse' type of person is likely to be quiet and methodical, a conscientious administrator who likes to get things right. A predominantly 'Bond' person is likely to be open with emotions and conscious of the importance of other people, a visible carer with individuals or inside a team. A 'Command' person is likely to be impatient for results and to know instinctively what needs doing, an entrepreneur or 'born organizer'.

But people rarely fit a style description exactly. People are usually a mixture of the three styles, generally of just two of them. *Few of us have the capacity to spread equally across all three.* We often have one which is an area of weakness which tends to ruin our all-round performance, but which can provide a useful focus for our personal development.

There are of course many current methods of identifying personal style. Generally, though, they provide you with an interesting profile but no *plan of action* to aid your development, and almost certainly no links to learnable management skills.

However, one of the benefits of the 'toolkit' approach is that the skills within the toolkit can be re-assembled into different shapes for different purposes. The skills in the Personal Development Toolkit on page 31 have been re-assembled to match the most appropriate style.

'Analyse' covers the *information*- providing skills ('monitoring', 'clarifying', 'specifying' and 'focusing'), skills associated with individual thinking processes.

'Bond' covers skills associated with being with *people* ('making more of others' ideas', 'giving and receiving feedback', 'communicating' and 'meeting'), skills most effective when done with openness and feeling.

The 'Command' skills are all related to taking *action* and getting results ('persuading', 'planning action', 'making decisions' and 'developing performance').

In the style questionnaire on pages 32 and 33 you are asked to consider yourself in relation to 12 straightforward statements. How far does each statement represent a fair description of you? Circle the appropriate number against each statement, and then circle the number in the next column to indicate the extent to which you would like to change the rating you have given yourself.

At the centre of the personal development model opposite are the core skills of 'specifying targets and standards', 'making more of others' ideas' and 'planning action' (in italics). These are the essence of the integrated style – **'Drive'** – which contains elements of the other three styles. It is the basis of a balanced *leadership* – and of an effective management – style:

Clear and positive in thinking towards future possibilities; capable of generating enthusiasm and a flexible approach to achieving results; is sensitive to others' feelings and expectations and inspires teamwork.

'Drive' style requires the ability to move between 'Head', 'Heart' and 'Feet', to be able to adjust your personal style according to the changing needs of the situation.

Personal Development Toolkit

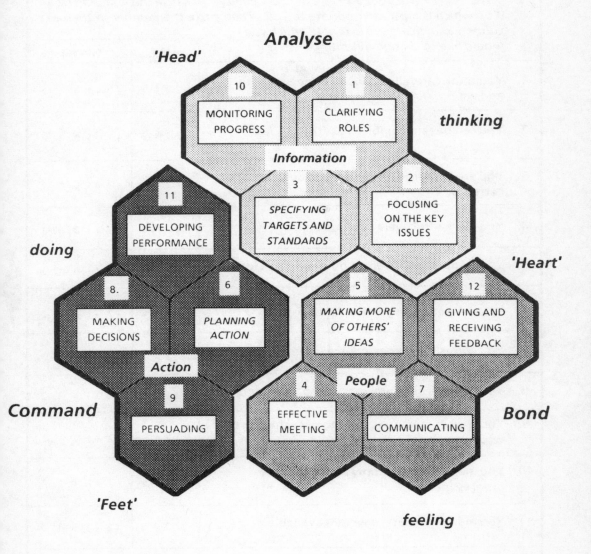

Style Questionnaire

3.1 Score the extent to which the following statements apply to you NOW on a scale 1–5 (1 = Not you; 3 = Yes, but...; 5 = Fully you). Circle the number (1 2 3 4 5) which is most appropriate to you. Then circle the number in the next column to indicate the extent to which you would like to change this rating:

		'NOW'	'CHANGE'
1.	You think carefully about what needs doing and why.	1 2 3 **4** 5	+2 +1 **0** -1 -2
2.	You can be relied upon to get things into perspective.	1 2 3 **4** 5	+2 +1 **0** -1 -2
3.	You are concerned that things should be done correctly.	1 2 3 **4** 5	+2 +1 **0** -1 -2
4.	You work effectively in groups.	1 2 3 **4** 5	+2 +1 **0** -1 -2
5.	You respond positively to other people's ideas.	1 2 3 4 **5**	+2 +1 0 **-1** -2
6.	You get people organized for action.	1 2 **3** 4 5	+2 **+1** 0 -1 -2
7.	You consistently keep people informed.	1 2 **3** 4 5	+2 **+1** 0 -1 -2
8.	You have no difficulty making up your mind.	1 2 **3** 4 5	**+2** +1 0 -1 -2
9.	You always seem to be able to get others to do what you want.	1 **2** 3 4 5	**+2** +1 0 -1 -2
10.	You make sure you know how things are progressing.	1 2 **3** 4 5	+2 **+1** 0 -1 -2
11.	You make the most of what is available.	1 2 **3** 4 5	**+2** +1 0 -1 -2
12.	You prefer to deal with people face-to-face.	1 2 **3** 4 5	**+2** +1 0 -1 -2

Bold type represents the scores in the example on page 35.   © *PETER GRAINGER 1994*

3.2   To consider your own relationship to the three basic styles transfer your 'Now' scores and the 'Change' scores from the questionnaire according to the number of each statement.   Add up the total 'Now' scores and highlight the most significant 'Change' scores, keeping the two sets separate:

	'NOW' SCORES	'CHANGE' SCORES

'Analyse'

1. You think carefully about what needs doing and why.   [   ] *4*   [   ] *0*

3. You are concerned that things should be done correctly.   [   ] *4*   [   ] *0*

10. You make sure you know how things are progressing.   [   ] *3*   [   ] *+1*

2. You can be relied upon to get things into perspective.   [   ] *4*   [   ] *0*

TOTAL   [   ] *15*

'Bond'

7. You consistently keep people informed.   [   ] *4*   [   ] *+1*

12. You prefer to deal with people face-to-face.   [   ] *3*   [(*+2*)]

5. You respond positively to other people's ideas.   [   ] *5*   [   ] *-1*

4. You work effectively in groups.   [   ] *4*   [   ] *0*

TOTAL   [   ] *16*

'Command'

9. You always seem to be able to get others to do what you want.   [   ] *2*   [(*+2*)]

6. You get people organized for action.   [   ] *3*   [   ] *+1*

8. You have no difficulty making up your mind.   [   ] *3*   [(*+2*)]

11. You make the most of what is available.   [   ] *3*   [(*+2*)]

TOTAL   [   ] *11*

Example scores are in **bold type**; the resulting profile appears on Page 35.

4. Style profile

You should now have a total score for each style, but these totals do not tell you very much until you see them graphically in relation to each other. It is this inter-relationship that is important, not the size of the totals produced.

By transferring your total scores for 'Analyse', 'Bond' and 'Command' on to the model on page 37 your profile will normally emerge as a triangle with a 'pull' towards one particular area of skills.

In the example opposite the person's *strengths* lie top right towards 'Analyse' and 'Bond' (AB and BA). The skills in that area are 'specifying targets and standards', 'focusing on the key issues', and 'making more of others' ideas'. The area on the *opposite* side to the shape of the profile (shaded) covers skills from CB to CA. These are likely to be among the skills to concentrate on as personal development priorities. 'Persuading' and 'making decisions' are covered in this workbook.

If the triangle of your profile is equilateral you are probably 'Drive' style, or at least have the potential to be. But it is more likely that there will be a 'pull' in one particular direction, a 'skew' towards one style or perhaps two. This skew will be in the direction of your *natural* strengths, and the skills on the model *nearest* to that skew will identify a particular area of confidence and competence for you.

Example of Completed Style Profile

4.1 Write your total 'Now' scores for each 'style' from 3.2 on page 33 in the boxes below:

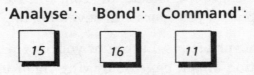

'Analyse':   'Bond':   'Command':

| 15 | 16 | 11 |

Circle or cross the appropriate number on the model below, and join up the points to produce a style profile. Then highlight the skills with the highest 'Change' scores:

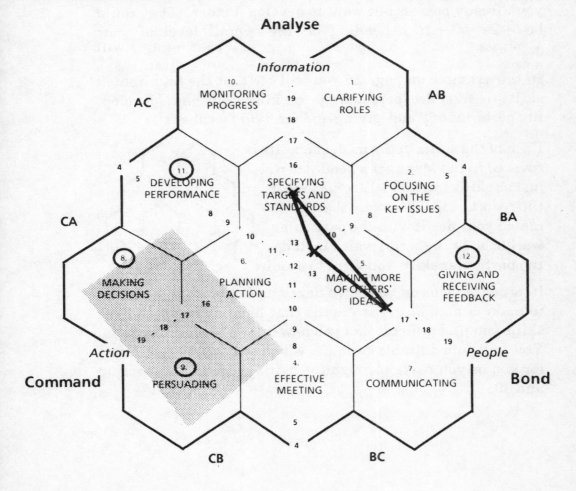

The skills on the model *furthest away* from the shape of your profile are those that you probably do not find easy to carry out; you may therefore need to concentrate on them particularly as part of your personal development.

To check out your priorities, highlight your highest 'Change' scores from Section 3.2 on page 33 by ringing or underlining the appropriate number on the model opposite. These may be skills which you find difficult and want to improve or skills you already possess but want to develop further. (They could be +2s or +1s depending on the overall level of your scoring.)

In the example on page 35 you will see that the highlighted skills (ie +2s) are 'persuading', 'making decisions', 'developing performance' and 'giving and receiving feedback'

Each of the skills in the model opposite is covered in the Manager's Toolkit series, just as skills 8, 9 and 10 are covered in this workbook. You can therefore match your needs with the particular workbook in the series which includes the particular skills you want to acquire.

In order to focus on your own development plan, it is helpful to make a note of the strengths that have emerged and the skills you find difficult that you now intend to concentrate on. You will find suitable formats, which will act as reminders for you as you move through the skills sections, on pages 38 and 39.

Style Profile

4.2 Write your total 'Now' scores for each 'style' from 3.2 on page 33 in the boxes below:

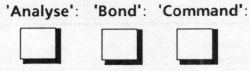

'Analyse':   **'Bond'**:   **'Command'**:

Circle or cross the appropriate number on the model below, and join up the points to produce a style profile. Then highlight the skills with the highest 'Change' scores:

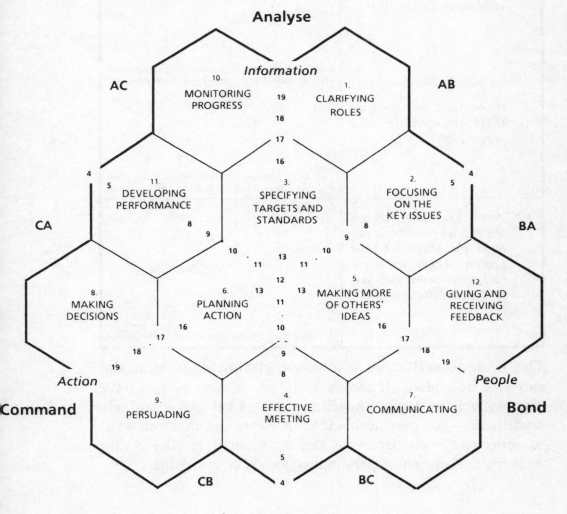

Analyse

Information

AC   10.
MONITORING
PROGRESS   19   1.
CLARIFYING
ROLES   AB

18

17

16

4   5
11.
DEVELOPING
PERFORMANCE   3.
SPECIFYING
TARGETS AND
STANDARDS   2.
FOCUSING
ON THE
KEY ISSUES   5   4

CA   8   8   BA

9   9

10   13   10
11   11
12
8.
MAKING
DECISIONS   6.   13
PLANNING
ACTION   13   5.
MAKING MORE
OF OTHERS'
IDEAS   12.
GIVING AND
RECEIVING
FEEDBACK

11

16   10   16   17

17   9   18

18   8   19

19   *Action*   *People*

Command   9.
PERSUADING   4.
EFFECTIVE
MEETING   7.
COMMUNICATING   **Bond**

5

CB   4   BC

© PETER GRAINGER 1994

From consideration of your profile, identify your strongest skills in the space below and consider ways of developing them. Then make a note of the skills furthest away from the shape of your profile, and confirm that these are the skills you want to improve.

4.3 Write down the skills closest to the shape of your profile which you also scored highly. These are your natural strengths: *How could you develop these strengths in your present job?*	*Specifying targets and standards, making more of other's ideas and focusing on the key issues* *Be more involved with strategy and developing ideas for departmental improvement*
4.4 Write down the skills on the model furthest away from the shape of your profile. These are likely to be the skills that you find most difficult:	*Making decisions, persuading and planning action*

The 'Change' skills that you have highlighted on the model can also be added. If they are the same ones as you have already written down, underline them as being particularly significant – you may decide that these are the ones you want to concentrate on first. In the example it is likely that 'making decisions and 'persuading' would be priorities.

4.4 (continued) Add the high-lighted 'Change' skills, underlining any on page 38 that are the same: *How committed are you to improving these skills?*	*Giving and receiving feedback and developing performance* *I've had no experience of counselling and developing staff and need skills to give me confidence*

5. MCI and Personal Competence

The MCI's Dimensions of Personal Competence correlate closely with the Personal Development Toolkit, and add another useful dimension to the conclusions you come to about yourself (see the integrated model on page 40):

> Monitoring, collecting and organizing information, identifying concepts and setting objectives are clearly competences relevant to *Analyse* characteristics.

> Showing sensitivity, managing personal emotions, presenting oneself positively and relating to others all match *Bond* traits.

> Obtaining commitment, taking decisions, managing personal development and showing self-confidence and personal drive are all associated with *Command* behaviour.

You can check your profile from page 37 with the *dimensions* of personal competence closest and furthest away from its shape on the model on page 40.

Personal Development and MCI's Dimensions of Personal Competence

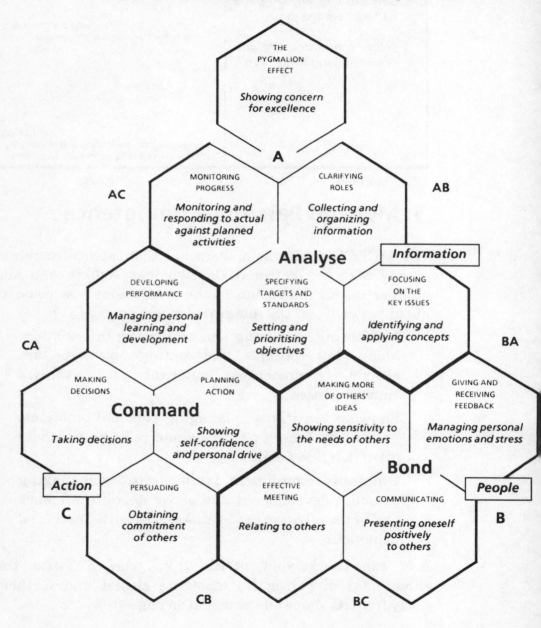

© PETER GRAINGER 1994

Chapter Two

MAKING DECISIONS

MAKING DECISIONS

Making decisions enables you to make a systematic selection between specific and significant resource alternatives.

1.   What's it for?

Managing resources frequently means making a decision between alternative resources. We cannot have them both, so we have to select *one* of them. So when we make decisions we are making a definite choice between discrete alternatives and *rejecting* those that do not meet our specification.

This is different from determining *priorities* when we are simply giving greater priority to one option rather than another. *All* of the options are likely to be dealt with – eventually. Often we combine options to create a plan by building this action with that. There can be no combinations in decision-making, one only is selected

This is why it is very important to have a systematic process for deciding *which* resource. However, for the process to be worth the time investment the choice needs to involve significant resources or important and distinct courses of action.

This often applies as much to decisions to be made outside the working environment as to those within it. At home we are more emotionally involved and are *personally* responsible – at work we often have only *shared* responsibility.

The first discipline is to be clear on the *purpose* of our decision, what we are trying to achieve as a result of making

1. What's it for?

Are you clear about the purpose of the decisions you have to make?

1.1 Think of a significant decision you will have to make shortly (or one which you made very recently). Describe the choice that you will have (or had) to make:	*Choose a family car to replace the Vauxhall*
1.2 What should be the result of this decision? *Write down what you intend to achieve by making this particular selection:*	*We shall have a replacement car that will get me to work, transport the family and enable us to camp in the summer*
1.3 How have you identified all available possible alternatives for you to consider when making this decision?	*Bought 'What Car?'; asked friends for recommendations*

the decision. Are we choosing a car primarily for work or for our annual family holiday? Am I the only one going to use the computer or do I have to recognize other people's requirements? Am I selecting a secretary or a personal assistant? As soon as we have a perspective on the purpose of our decision, we have limited the range – and so the potential confusion – of the alternatives going into the top of our decision-making filter-system.

Indeed until we have a clear understanding of our decision *purpose* we cannot identify the valid alternatives. Alternative cars for family holidays will be very different from a car primarily required to get the bread-winner to and from work every day.

Before any decision-making takes place a systematic survey of *all* valid alternatives should be undertaken. It must not be assumed that the options that *immediately* spring to mind are those that will automatically produce the best ultimate selection. We need to be as systematic and open-minded in looking for possible alternatives *before* we start the process as we are in filtering those alternatives later.

Making decisions is about putting a series of filters into the funnel of the process that will ultimately leave us with just one 'best buy' from all the options that are available at the beginning. Obviously the better the options going into the top, the better will be the final selection at the bottom.

Ideally one-by-one each alternative is filtered out by our criteria until only one clear 'winner' emerges. But we must be very *precise* in putting those filters in place – we can never know, for example, whether the person we rejected would have been better than the person we actually appointed.

1.4 List all the alternatives from which your choice will be made:	
1.5 Which of the alternatives do not meet the purpose statement you wrote down in Section 1.2, and why?	*Must be a hatchback - can't fit all our camping equipment in a boot, and estates are too expensive*
1.6 Are you quite certain you have carefully considered all the available alternatives that could satisfy your purpose? *What further action could you take to make sure you have not overlooked anything or anyone?*	*Check in 'Yellow Pages' for list of dealers, and visit all reputable ones to see for myself*

2. Placing the filters

The key step in any systematic decision-making is the selection of criteria, the filters to be placed in the funnel. The first and most important criteria are the fixed filters, the *essential* or minimum standards which every alternative *must* meet. If any alternative does not meet any of them, it is automatically rejected.

The essential criteria have to be very carefully considered so that there are not so many of them that they cut off the supply of options entirely, nor so unspecific that every option is permitted to pass through. There are unlikely to be more than three or four.

The best way to select criteria is to list out all the *possible* criteria relevant to your decision purpose, and then to highlight those that are essential. Since any alternative that does not meet that standard is rejected, it is critical that each essential criterion can be measured.

If the measurement is vague the filter simply gives way as each alternative comes in contact with it. If, for example, we say every member of the family must approve the choice of car how are we going to *measure* that approval?

Moreover, essential must mean the *minimum*, if it is to be the means of rejecting alternatives outright. If we really can't afford to spend more than £7000, *we must reject* every car that costs over that price – and are extras included?

You should be able to test your options against these measurable minimum criteria quite easily on a 'yes' or 'no' basis. They either meet the standards or they do not; if they do not, reject them at this point. Ideally you should then have *two or three* alternatives to take on to the final stage. If you

2. Placing the filters

Are you clear about the criteria on which you are going to base the decision?

2.1 Write down all the criteria or standards against which you think you might be judging the alternatives:

Cost, capacity, economy, comfort, reliability...

2.2 Identify those criteria that are essential, the minimum standards you will accept:

Are they all measurable? If they are not, either rewrite them or reject them as essential criteria:

Room for push-chair/tents; spouse likes; cost £7000 max, 1400cc min

Hatchback; spouse happy driving; £7000 total - £2000 part exchange

2.3 List the measurable essential criteria on the Decision Worksheet on page 54, and then check whether each alternative meets those criteria on a 'yes' or 'no' basis.

Place a tick or cross on the matrix under the respective column. Your shortlist will consist only of those alternatives that meet all the essential criteria.

have more than that number you will need to add the non-essential or *desirable* criteria as additional filters to the funnel.

The desirable criteria enable us to cut out more options until we are left with a shortlist of just two or three. We do this by listing the options in descending order of importance from high priority to low. Having put them in order, score each alternative on 1–10 scale against the *high* priority criteria, on a 1–7 scale for the *medium* and 1–4 for the *low* priority criteria.

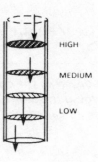

The full decision-making process involves giving a weighting factor to each of the desirable criteria and then multiplying the scores for each alternative against that factor. But this step tends to make the process particularly complicated and time-consuming. It is also difficult to arrive at the correct balance between factors of similar type.

3. Reaching a conclusion

The alternatives that have come through the scoring process may well now have little to choose between them, and that is no bad thing. It is as well not to rely too heavily on the accuracy of the final score of a systematic scoring system. It can also be very limiting to have only *one* final selection – the car may have been sold or the candidate accepted a job elsewhere.

To choose the final 'best buy', we introduce a more subtle tool, weighing up the relative *advantages* and *disadvantages* of each.

2.4 If you still have more than three alternatives to choose between, list the desirable criteria from 2.1, ranking them 'High', 'Medium' or 'Low' in terms of priority:

Check exactly what you mean by each and then add them to the Worksheet.

2.5 Using the Worksheet, score each remaining alternative on a scale 1-10 for the 'High' priority criteria, 1-7 for the 'Medium' and 1-4 for the 'Low'. Total the scores for each alternative and identify the two or three highest.

3. Reaching a conclusion

Can you systematically choose between the remaining two or three alternatives?

3.1 List the two or three highest scoring alternatives:

1:

2:

3:

1: Peugeot 205; 2: Citroen BX

This step is what you would tend to do if you had only two (or possibly three) options to choose between in the first place. Often a decision is simply a question of the choice between taking action and *not* taking action, a 'binary' decision. Considering the *advantages and disadvantages* of doing something and then of *not* doing it is quick and effective; it does not call for the full systematic approach.

List all the advantages and disadvantages of each of the final alternatives you can think of on the Decision Worksheet on pages 54-5. Highlight the most significant. The choice will now be a question of comparing one or two key *advantages* against one or two key *disadvantages*.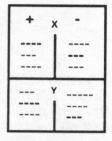

The final choice is made by referring back to your purpose statement and the list of criteria and determining which of the key advantages or disadvantages is the most critical to you.

Remember that disadvantages can be overcome and advantages exploited (see 'Focusing on the Key Issues' in Volume 3 of the *Managers' Toolkit* series). You might actually be able to overcome a major disadvantage of your *second* choice which could then emerge as your 'best buy'.

The full systematic decision-making process is a very valuable tool when you have a very important decision to make (eg a high cost resource) with numerous alternatives and many criteria to consider. Normally decisions are required in much less formal – and less time-consuming – situations, and in those situations a quick reference to the *pros and cons* of each is quite adequate.

Whichever method is used, both are usually preferable to the 'gut feel', instant selection, that works well in an emergency but seems to be considered the norm for 'proactive' managers.

3.2 List the advantages and disadvantages of each of the remaining alternatives on the Decision Worksheet, highlighting the most significant:

3.3 Consider these factors against the purpose and criteria: Can you think of ways of overcoming the disadvantage of one or exploiting the advantage of another?

As a result, what is your final decision and why?

Peugeot 205 - it's easier to handle, safer and economical. Don't need extra space (or depreciation!) until children are older

3.4 Write down a 'binary' ('yes' or 'no') decision situation you have to face (or one you have recently faced):

Do we need to buy a new copier?

3.5 List the advantages and disadvantages of each alternative, underlining the most significant: Does the right decision emerge as a result?

ADVANTAGES OF ALTERNATIVE A

A

Buy

DISADVANTAGES OF ALTERNATIVE A

More facilities, fewer breakdowns, better image

Present model OK, short of capital, retraining

ADVANTAGES OF ALTERNATIVE B

B

Don't buy

Retrain staff on current model

DISADVANTAGES OF ALTERNATIVE B

Capital needed elsewhere, staff familiarity...

Staff's attitude, present machine won't last...

DECISION WORKSHEET	ALTERNATIVES:						
	C	PEUGEOT		VAUXHALL			D
	B	RENAULT			CITROEN		E
ESSENTIAL CRITERIA:	A	TOYOTA				FIAT	F
Hatchback		✓	✓	✓	✓	✓	✓	Tick or
1400 cc minimum		✓	✓	✓	✓	✓	✓	cross
Total cost no more than £6000 less part exchange £2000 min.		✗	✓	✓	✓	✓	✓	each
Spouse happy driving this model		✓	✓	✓	✗	✓	✓	option:

DESIRABLE CRITERIA in order of importance:	A	B	C	D	E	F	SCALE:
1. Economical in traffic	✗	5	6	✗	3	3	
2. Comfortable to drive		6	8		9	6	HIGH 1-10
3.							
4. Reliability		3	4		5	2	
5. Net cost		4	4		5	6	MED 1-7
6. Relatively low mileage/cost		4	6		4	3	
7. Both like design and colour		6	5		7	3	
8.							
9. Location of servicing		3	2		3	3	LOW 1-4
10. Ventilation		2	3		1	2	
Score each alternative on H, M or L scale: TOTAL:		33	38		37	28	TOP SCORES

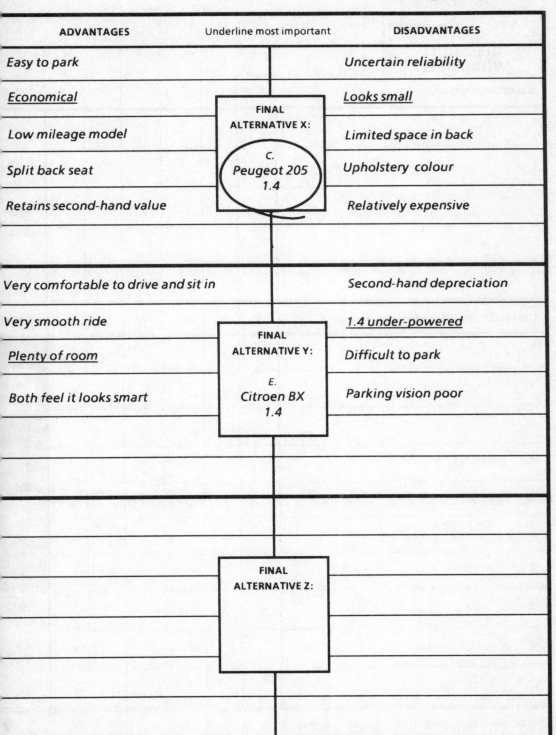

ADVANTAGES	Underline most important	DISADVANTAGES
Easy to park		Uncertain reliability
Economical	**FINAL**	_Looks small_
Low mileage model	**ALTERNATIVE X:**	Limited space in back
Split back seat	C. Peugeot 205 1.4	Upholstery colour
Retains second-hand value		Relatively expensive
Very comfortable to drive and sit in		Second-hand depreciation
Very smooth ride	**FINAL**	_1.4 under-powered_
Plenty of room	**ALTERNATIVE Y:**	Difficult to park
Both feel it looks smart	E. Citroen BX 1.4	Parking vision poor
	FINAL	
	ALTERNATIVE Z:	

ALTERNATIVES:	C				D
DECISION WORKSHEET	B				E
ESSENTIAL CRITERIA:	A				F

						Tick or
						cross
						each
						option:

DESIRABLE CRITERIA in order of importance:	A	B	C	D	E	F	SCALE:
1.							
2.							HIGH 1-10
3.							
4.							
5.							MED 1-7
6.							
7.							
8.							
9.							LOW 1-4
10.							
Score each alternative on H, M or L scale: TOTAL:							TOP SCORES

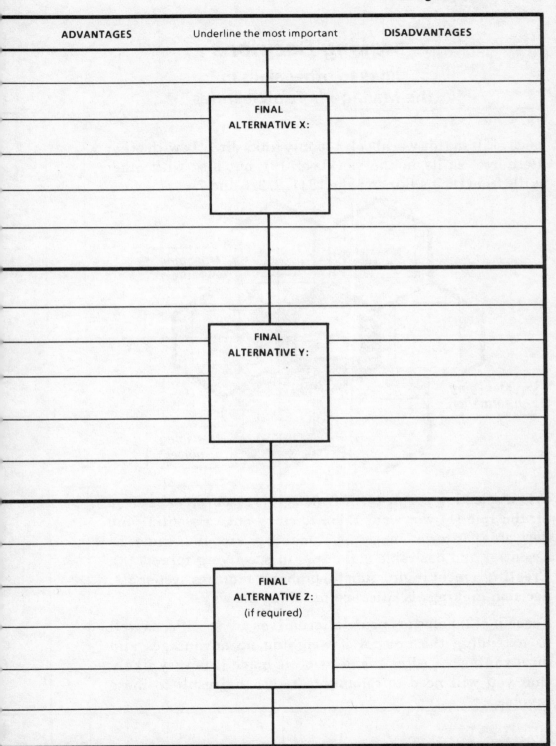

ADVANTAGES   Underline the most important   DISADVANTAGES

FINAL
ALTERNATIVE X:

FINAL
ALTERNATIVE Y:

FINAL
ALTERNATIVE Z:
(if required)

Making Decisions
links to other skills in
the Manager's Toolkit series

Each skill in this workbook not only links directly with other 'Resource' skills in the workbook (9), but also with other skills from the toolkit on page 13 (1, 2, 3, 6 and 7).

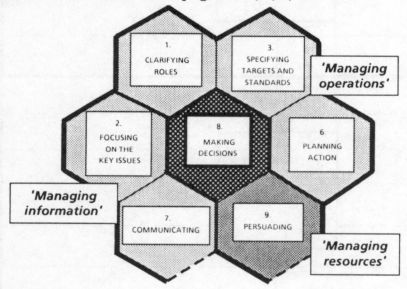

When selecting people *(MCI Unit 4)* it is essential to be clear on the role (1) you want them to carry out. Essential and desirable criteria in decision-making are the same as essential and desirable *standards* in specifying targets (3). Creating a meaningful plan (6) probably requires systematic decision-making at critical points along the way.

Focusing (2) helps to ensure alternatives are specific, as well as extending the process of weighing up advantages and disadvantages. After the decision is made it is very likely that you will need to communicate (7) the result to those involved.

Chapter Three

PERSUADING

Chapter Three

PERSUADING

Persuading helps you to get people to do what they may not otherwise want to do.

1. Preparing the message

Frequently when managing resources we have to get other people to agree to things that they would prefer not to agree to. When resources are seriously constrained, persuading may become *negotiating*. I shall not be covering that specialist skill in depth, although there are many overlaps with effective negotiating in the approach I shall be advocating.

Persuading is getting someone to do something specific that they are unlikely to want to do – persuasion is not required if they respond readily to what we want them to do.

First we have to be very clear in our own mind exactly what it is we want done. The clearer we are on our *purpose and objective* the more effective we shall be as persuaders. This usually means defining the end result we want to come as a result of the persuasion, including the minimum standards we are prepared to accept (see 'Specifying Targets and Standards' in Volume 1 of the *Manager's Toolkit* series).

It not only helps us to have a clear picture of our purpose and objective before us, but also helps the person we are trying to persuade. Most of us are more inclined to go along with what someone else wants if we know *why* they want it. We need to have a perspective on the requirement, an understanding of why it is important, and where it fits into our own scheme of things.

1. Preparing the message

Are you quite clear what you are trying to persuade the other person to do?

1.1 Think of a situation in which you want someone to do something that he/she may not want to do:	*Get Fred Evans to accept my taking over Bill's section*
1.2 Write down the purpose of your persuasion? What do you want the other person to do or not do?	*To stop complaining to other members of the section*
1.3 What do you want to tell the other person by way of explanation? Write down the minimum message you want to get across:	*More security in combined section, overlaps are inefficient*

The starting point for persuasion, then, is to make clear with a simple message *why* you want something done. The message needs to be clear and brief so that it is easily understood and so that both of you can keep it in mind as the discussion proceeds.

However, *logic is not necessarily persuasive* – people do not always respond rationally! You may put up a very well prepared and reasonable case, only for the other person to dismiss it on totally illogical grounds. The more information you present, the easier it is for the other person to find a weak link in the chain and cut it.

You need to give careful thought to the *person* you are trying to persuade. Is he or she the real decision-maker? What sort of person is he or she? Will he need a detailed explanation, or will he want you to come straight to the point? Is she likely to be sensitive to pressure or enjoy the cut-and-thrust of an argument? How is he likely to *react* to what you are proposing?

As a result of these considerations you need to think *how* you are going to do the persuading. Must it be face-to-face or could you do it by phone? Will you be persuading on your own; if not, what will be the effect of the others? Do you need a carefully prepared plan or should you keep it informal?

As with 'communicating', you should be careful what language you use. Particularly when seeking approval for *specialist* resources (*MCI Unit 3*), you may be inclined to use specialist jargon with which others may be unfamiliar. You may need some form of visual or other aid to help you get your message across. If you need visual aids to persuade a *group of people,* it is probable that your persuading situation has become a *presentation,* and as such the contents of this chapter is equally relevant.

1.4 What sort of person(s) are you trying to persuade?	
	Long-service, particularly loyal to Bill, obstinate
How is he or she likely to react to what you are proposing?	
	He won't be listening; will show he's not interested
1.5 How are you planning to get the message across?	
	Start by discussing his job in new section, try to develop rapport before moving on to his complaining
What sort of language will be appropriate?	
	Keep it simple, speak slowly, keep asking him questions
Would any sort of aid help to make an impact?	
	No - counter-productive for Fred
1.6 Will you be alone? If not what will be the effect of the other person(s)?	
	No - it must be one-to-one - he'd switch off with others

2. Creating the climate

The other person is more likely to agree to what you want if he can see some benefit to himself. It is therefore very important to give some thought to *his or her* objectives or interests. If they are the same as yours you are unlikely to have much difficulty reaching agreement.

But what do you know of the other person's objectives? Do you need to ask someone closer to him? Are his interests likely to be prejudiced by what you are proposing? Are you going to be able to build *common ground* between you?

A positive, friendly atmosphere helps enormously to persuade, and yet, especially if resistance is anticipated, the initial climate of any persuasion situation is often tense and confrontational. It is very important not to give the impression that you are *anticipating* a hostile response – 'You're not going to like this, Fred, but...!' (see the Pygmalion Effect on page 24).

Pick the place for the discussion carefully. Are you likely to be interrupted? Is neutral territory likely to help? Try to sit next to the person, rather than opposite him or her. Some form of refreshment will usually help to relax you both. A welcoming smile generally reassures – provided it is genuine!

Once the discussion starts the use of *questions* is critical. The sooner you can ask a question of him the quicker the atmosphere will relax. He will not really be listening until he has had an opportunity to contribute to the discussion himself, and so he must be involved, rather than talked *at*, as quickly as possible. Ask how he feels about the proposal you have just made. Does he appreciate the importance? Has he had a similar experience?

2. Creating the climate

How are you going to create a climate favourable to persuasion?

2.1 *Do you think you have any objectives or interests in common with the person you are going to persuade?*	
	Company loyalty & long-service
How could you make the most of any objectives or interests you have in common?	
	Share concern for the future of the business - his pension!
2.2 *Have you chosen the most suitable location to put you both at ease?*	
	He knows my office - anywhere else would be artificial - but I'll sit his side of the desk
How could you relax the atmosphere at the beginning, and make sure that he or she is actually listening?	
	Explain purpose of meeting in context of business needs
What sort of questions could you ask to help create a positive climate?	
	Ask him to tell me about his concerns

Persuasion is very personal. We tend to be persuaded by people we like and not by people we do not. Why is it that we buy from some people and not from others? It's not just a question of price!

You need to build a *personal relationship*, a rapport, which will make it difficult for the other person to refuse what you are requesting. What do the two of you have in common? What do you like about him? Could you build on that commonality, or the aspect of his personality that you like?

Having created a more positive climate for persuasion you will be in a much better position to *develop* the common ground, the common objectives, that should emerge between you as you talk. If you are constantly on the look-out for what *unites* you rather than what divides you, you will be surprised just how much will emerge.

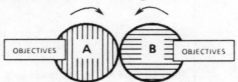

After all this positive preparation, you are now in a better position to consider what could go wrong, what aspects he might *not* agree to. Having considered the potential 'pros', you are now confident enough to think about the potential 'cons', the risks that exist to your successful persuasion (see 'Planning Action' in Volume 1, 'Managing Operations').

Because the need to *persuade* anticipates resistance we are often inclined to over-emphasise the risks at the beginning and so diminish our confidence. We can now calmly address the likelihood of each risk coming about and the impact on our objectives if it did.

2.3 Could you build a personal rapport with this person, and if so, how?	
	I respect his experience and loyalty to Bill
2.4 Considering your purpose in 1.2, what area of common ground can you envisage emerging between you?	
	Compatible work of our two sections, appreciation of expertise, Company commitment
2.5 What are the main risks to a successful outcome?	*He could become personal or refuse to listen*
How could you minimise the likelihood and the impact?	*Be careful not to react, don't argue, try to stay friendly but firm*

3. Considering style

Personal style is critical to persuading. The subtle 'chemistry' of one person trying to persuade another is quite as important as the arguments prepared or the skills deployed. Consideration of personal style is not only relevant to the way the persuader and the persuaded are likely to behave as individuals, but also to how one person's style will impact on another's.

For example two 'Analyse' people will behave very differently towards each other from two 'Command' people, and an 'Analyse' person persuading a 'Command', 'Bond' an 'Analyse', etc, etc – the implications are considerable.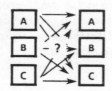

It is worth the effort involved in considering how the different styles are likely to affect the behaviour of both the persuader and the persuaded. In preparing for a persuading situation consider the likely behaviour of both of you with the help of the checklist in Section 3.1 (pages 68–9).

The scoring, 'High', 'Medium' and 'Low' relates to the likelihood of the particular behaviour happening in the particular persuading situation you have in mind. Complete the checklist and then consider how to overcome the possible weaknesses and exploit the possible strengths that may have emerged.

Of course there will be occasions when, as the person responsible for the resource being discussed, you may have to insist on your objective being met – 'Command' style, 'managers' right to manage' etc. If all your attempts at reasonable persuasion fail, you may simply have to give an order to get the job done.

However, giving orders without the commitment of the ordered, is likely to be a very short-term, emergency solution. The job may get done, but without enthusiasm and without quality performance.

Often we do not have the power or the authority simply to give an order. Very often in trying to manage (and acquire) resources we are persuading colleagues and bosses. In this situation we have to be much more skilful, becoming masters of 'Drive' style, working *with* the other person (see page 30) instead of against him or her.

Ideally you are trying to achieve a situation in which *both* parties are able to appreciate the benefits of what is being proposed, creating a *'win/win'* situation for you both. If your relationship is *long-term*, you are both more likely to see the importance of *both* of you being satisfied with the result.

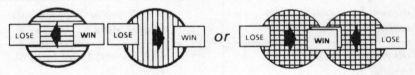

If there is no win-win situation, for every person who is seen to have 'won' in the short-term another has been created who has 'lost'. The 'loser' will then make every effort to 'get even' with the other person at some time in the future. With long-term relationships you would be sensible not to take that risk!

It is therefore important that in planning to persuade you know the other person well enough to be able to adjust *what* you are going to say and *how* you are going to say it in a manner that is attractive to the style and nature of the particular person being persuaded.

3. Considering style

Do you think personal style could affect the success of your planned persuasion?

3.1   Based on your style profile on Page 12 and your view of the other person in Section 1.4, consider the style implications of what could happen. Score the likelihood of you or the other person behaving in the manner described, 'H' = very likely to happen; 'M' = could well happen; 'L' = unlikely to happen:

AS THE PERSUADER:		*Analyse*	AS THE PERSUADED:	
You will be clear what you want to happen.	H		He/she will be quite clear on his/her own position.	H
You will have produced a carefully argued case.	M		He will produce a carefully argued reply.	L
You want to be fair and reasonable.	H		He will want to be fair and reasonable.	L
You are likely to clarify and not react to what the other person says.	M		He is likely to clarify and not react to what you say.	L
		Bond		
You will want to be cooperative and to see his point of view.	M		He will want to be cooperative and to see your point of view.	L
You will want to be able to reach an amicable agreement.	H		He will want to reach an amicable agreement.	M
You will not want to push too hard for a conclusion.	M		He will not want to push his point of view too hard.	M
You may react if things don't go smoothly.	M		He may react if things don't go smoothly.	H

AS THE PERSUADER:	*Command*	AS THE PERSUADED:
You will make it very clear what you want.	M	He will make it very clear what he wants.	L
You will have confidence in your ability to get him to do what you want.	M	He will have confidence in his ability to get you to do what he wants.	(L)
You are unlikely to pause to clarify what he has said.	M	He is unlikely to pause to clarify what you have said.	(L)
You will push for a result which is to your advantage.	M	He will push for a result which is to his advantage.	M

3.2 As a result of your scoring, highlight the key areas for attention.

What action could you take to ensure a more successful outcome?

I need to keep discussion factual, fair and friendly - allow plenty of pauses; I mustn't threaten his confidence

3.3 Do you have the prospect of a long-term relationship with this person?

Unless he takes early retirement! We can work together if he will cooperate. If he leaves, I shall have 'failed'

3.4 How far are you now able to anticipate a 'win-win' outcome?

He's got plenty to offer and we need his experience; as far as I know he needs to go on working

PERSUADING QUESTIONNAIRE

Think back to the last time you had to persuade someone to do something they did not want to do and consider how effective you were:

1. What was the purpose of the persuasion?	*For Fred Evans to accept my taking over Bill's section and to stop complaining about the re-organization to the rest of the section.*
How successful were you in the short-term. Do you think you will also be successful in the long-term?	*Fred Evans has stopped complaining to other members of the section and understands the reasons for the organisation change. We should be able to use his experience in time. Time and patience will bring him round.*
2. What was the minimum message you wanted to get across and how well did you do it?	*That there will be more security for everyone in the combined department and confirm my respect for Bill's expertise.*
	I 'told' him rather than getting points out gradually, but he was listening and I think my enthusiasm for Bill's work was convincing.
3. How effective was your use of questioning?	*Because he didn't react at all at the start, I talked too much about his work in the new section. But asking him about his real concerns and letting him get it off his chest worked well.*
4. How far were you able to exploit and develop the common objectives, common interests or common ground that emerged between you?	*His loyalty to the Company – and to Bill – was soon apparent, so I was able to share that commitment. Talking about the common work of the two sections gave us common ground to build on, but he may have seen it as a management 'technique'!*

5.	How far were you able to build a personal rapport in the course of the discussion?	*Although he was still a little 'delicate' and didn't seem very enthusiastic about ways of using his experience in the new section, I think he was secretly pleased to know that his experience was appreciated and would be made use of.*
6.	Did the risks that you anticipated arise, and how well were you able to deal with them?	*He was difficult at the beginning, but the strategy of not arguing or reacting to any provocation worked very well. He listened more than I expected and warmed slowly as we talked.*
7.	How far did personal style play a part?	*He was initially too on edge to behave normally, but his 'Bond' style came out later and helped our rapport. I think my 'Analyse' and 'Bond' helped me to balance warmth with sense.*
	Did you both behave as you had anticipated?	*It did go much as I had expected - at least at the beginning.*
8.	If you were to persuade that person again what would you do differently to be more effective?	*I don't think I made enough allowance for him to recover in the course of the discussion – perhaps higher expectations of a more positive outcome ('Pygmalion Effect') would have helped.*

PERSUADING QUESTIONNAIRE

Think back to the last time you had to persuade someone to do something they did not want to do and consider how effective you were:

1. What was the purpose of the persuasion? How successful were you in the short-term. Do you think you will also be successful in the long-term?	
2. What was the minimum message you wanted to get across and how well did you do it?	
3. How effective was your use of questioning?	
4. How far were you able to exploit and develop the common objectives, common interests or common ground that emerged between you?	

5. How far were you able to build a personal rapport in the course of the discussion?	
6. Did the risks that you anticipated arise, and how well were you able to deal with them?	
7. How far did personal style play a part? Did you both behave as you had anticipated?	
8. If you were to persuade that person again what would you do differently to be more effective?	

Persuading
links to other skills in
the Manager's Toolkit series

Each skill in this workbook not only links directly with other 'Resource' skills in the workbook (8), but also with other skills from the toolkit on page 13 (1, 3, 6, 7 and 12).

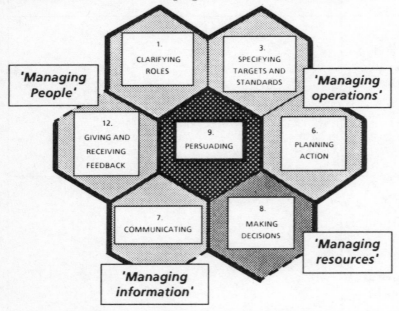

In giving 'operational' direction to others, from clarifying roles and targets (1 and 3) to planning action (6), there will be aspects of what has to be done that individuals will not want to do, and a requirement for resources/services which others will not want to provide, without persuasion.

Communicating a difficult business situation (7) may need an element of persuasion, while not all aspects of performance feedback (12) will be accepted by the person involved, who will therefore need to be persuaded of the performance improvement required.

Chapter Four

MONITORING PROGRESS

MONITORING PROGRESS

Monitoring progress provides you with the information to retain control over your resources, and to be able to handle effectively any problems that may arise

1.   Keeping in touch

The emphasis in *Managing Resources* is on making the most of the resources that we as managers have at our disposal. We cannot do that unless we are consistently in touch with how each of our resources is performing, whether they be people, equipment, systems or services.

It is therefore essential that we have in place methods of monitoring resources in such a way that we can know consistently whether or not we are getting a reasonable return on the investment the business is making in each of them.   As a customer for each, are we getting 'quality' performance? Are we confident in the progress of our *priority* tasks?

Methods of monitoring can be split between regular and special methods, and between direct and indirect methods. The most obvious *regular* and *direct* method is a team meeting (see 'Effective Meeting' in Volume 3, *Managing Information*) for groups, and appraisal or performance review (see 'Giving and Receiving Feedback' in Volume 2, *Managing People*) for individuals.

Special direct methods of monitoring, ie those to keep control of one-off objectives or special projects, are primarily individual or group *task reviews*.   They depend on the stand-

1. Keeping in touch

Do you know consistently how well your resources are performing?

1.1 Identify a priority task or a key on-going activity which one of your staff is performing:	*Section leaders to develop cost reduction ideas with their staff by 30 June*
1.2 How are you currently monitoring the progress of this task?	*Regular item on team meeting agenda*
1.3 How far are you monitoring progress directly yourself or indirectly through other people? **Should you do more personally?**	*Directly at meetings, but I don't know extent of staff's involvment. Will ask some informally*

very dependent on the standards you build into the special tasks when you set them up with your staff (see 'Specifying Targets and Standards' and 'Planning Action' in Volume 1, *Managing Operations*). Particular dates have to be programmed to ensure the task reviews actually take place.

These are the formal and direct management methods of monitoring, but we tend to use *informal and indirect* methods just as frequently. We ask other people's views on how well something or someone is working, which is often done in as haphazard a manner as a question in the lift or over a chat in the pub. How far can we trust the information we receive in this manner?

These days we have very sophisticated methods to help us know what is going on - *computers*! We can study printouts and spreadsheets, trend analyses and pie-charts; but are they really telling us how our resources are performing? Like the ubiquitous monthly report, not only do they depend on the 'garbage in, garbage out' syndrome, but are rarely up-to-date.

The more you can obtain information on the progress of your resources as a result of direct and *personal involvement* the better. There is no substitute for the manager being seen around – so long as there is a good reason for being there! Try to make a habit of getting out and about, however tied to your desk you may feel. See and *get a sense of* how things are going for yourself – 'get your antennae tuned!'

Monitoring in person can also be a creative management process – 'by exception' reporting certainly is not. Make sure people are aware of the *standards* to which they (and *their* resources) should be performing. Try to keep your contacts positive and show genuine interest in what is going on, as you ask questions and listen carefully to the replies you receive.

1.4 *How far are you monitoring this task through your regular methods?*	*Team meetings and monthly reports*
Should you arrange a method specially for this priority task?	*Yes - regular individual reviews of Section Leaders before end of June, and questioning staff personally*
1.5 *Identify your other on-going methods of monitoring progress:*	*Appraisal and counselling, spend v budget print-out, meetings with customers*
How confident are you of the value of the regular or systems reports that you receive?	*Monthly report with analyses is good discipline, but can put gloss on events. Print-out's delay*
1.6 *How often are you seen personally by your staff?*	*Pass most on way to meetings, but no time for informal contacts*
How could you improve your informal contact?	*Allocate half-an-hour a week to drop in*
How far do your staff feel responsible for monitoring their own performance?	*Have never really thought about it. I'll ask Section Leaders at next team meeting*

Enquire whether individuals have any suggestions for improvement, and encourage them to learn to monitor themselves. *Self-monitoring* – something we all do when we travel or play a game – can be both motivational and cost effective. It is also likely to be more accurate since people don't usually cheat themselves!

2. Is there a problem?

In monitoring progress, in checking that all is well, we are naturally conscious that we may have a problem – the essence of 'managing by exception'. A problem is usually something that is going wrong, a resource which is not as it should be. It is causing us concern, and, because it causes us concern, it is often difficult to be *objective* about the information that tells us about what is actually going wrong.

If we suspect something is wrong, assumptions are made, conclusions drawn and a balanced view of the situation hard to achieve. Often our perception of 'the problem' merely confirms our long-held view of a person, a situation or even a machine – 'not the copier again!' It is very easy to find ourselves with a self-fulfilling prophecy of failure. A single unsatisfactory incident can easily escalate into a crisis.

It is therefore essential that care is taken to obtain the necessary information relevant to each particular problem situation. You need to draw conclusions from the *facts* and not from assumptions. Have you actually seen the evidence for yourself or is it hearsay? Have you simply picked up the information you wanted to find and ignored any evidence to the contrary?

2. Is there a problem?

Do you think you have a problem?

2.1 *Think of a problem that you have at the moment. It is likely to be something you are concerned about and cannot see how to put right. Write it down as you now see it.*

> *Our most experienced clerk is no longer interested in the job - she's been here too long*

2.2 *What are the sources of information through which you have monitored this situation and from which you have now written this statement?*

> *Jane told me the analyses weren't ready; Jim reported her 'rudeness'*

2.3 *What additional information do you think you need and how will you get it?*

> *For how long have the analyses been late? How is her other paperwork? Ask Jim and Jane*

To make sure that you keep the analysis of any problem as systematic as possible try to see it in terms of the difference between what *should be* happening and what *is actually* happening, or, as the MCI put it in Element 3.2, 'actual or potential significant deviations from plan'.

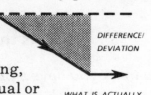

WHAT SHOULD
BE HAPPENING.

DIFFERENCE/
DEVIATION

WHAT IS ACTUALLY
HAPPENING.

There must be an identifiable difference between a situation which is 'wrong' and the standard which is 'right'. You must therefore have a clear idea of the target that is *not* being achieved *vis-a-vis* the result which is causing you concern.

So define the target or standard that is *not* being met. Is there a target with standards, and does everyone involved know of them? Are you precisely sure what is going wrong in comparison with the target or standards? As soon as you start to have the information, *write down* the problem to help you focus on the information you are missing.

3. Checking the evidence

You can now apply the basics of the systematic approach, questioning who? what? where? when? etc, to make sure you have not missed any critical piece of *evidence* (see 'Specifying Targets and Standards' in Volume 1, *Managing Operations*).

Who is not doing what they should be doing, or is doing what they should *not* be doing? Because people are so complex, problems with *people* are the most liable to misinterpretation. We become most emotional and least rational in dealing with problems relating to people. In such situations therefore we need to be particularly careful that we have got the *facts* behind what is actually going wrong.

2.4 Try to refine the problem statement you wrote in Section 2.1 as the difference between what should be happening and what is actually happening. Is there a target or standard which ought to be being met but which is not?

TARGET:

Margaret has a role clarification and knows the procedures and standards, ie to complete all analyses by the last Friday in the month, and to handle all phone queries without complaint

ACTUAL SITUATION:

Margaret's analyses for my monthly report arrive late and is said to be rude to people on the phone

3. Checking the evidence

Are you satisfied that you now know precisely what is going wrong so that you can take appropriate action to put it right?

3.1 Write down precisely <u>what</u> is not happening that should be happening (or vice versa), and <u>who</u> is or was involved. Consider <u>where</u> – it could be significant.

WHAT?

Analyses were not ready in time for my last two monthly reports. Jim has remarked on her rudenesss on the phone

WHO?

Margaret, reported by Jim, Jane and phone calls from sections of our department only

Having identified what's been done and who has been involved, it is often most helpful to identify *when* the problem came about. When was it first apparent? How long has it been a problem? Has it always been a problem, or is it starting to get worse now?

Often the timing of the problem will lead you to a significant cause, the key change, the straw that finally 'broke the camel's back'. Looking at the 'how much', the size of the problem and whether it is getting worse, will help to ensure that you are not trying to solve a problem that is really not very important.

The process of *questioning* makes sure that you are not jumping to false conclusions, *assuming* a person, a time, a place, when there is actually no evidence to support that assumption. It is better to take time checking the evidence than wasting time in solving the wrong problem or identifying the wrong cause.

Keep re-writing your statement of the problem as you gradually assemble the answers to the questions, until you finally have a statement that adequately expresses what is going wrong in terms of who, what, when, where etc. This re-writing may simply mean crossing out the odd word or phrase until what remains is the most precise *definition* of the problem that you can obtain.

Make sure that you have not avoided any key information. If you do not have the information, or if the evidence is not readily available, do your best to obtain it. How significant might it be if you could get hold of it? Are you prepared to proceed without it? Would it matter waiting until it becomes available? It is never easy to go looking for information that might cast doubt on your firmly held assumption!

3.2 When was the problem first apparent and how much of a problem is it now? Has it been getting worse?

> WHEN?
>
> *Reports for March and April; analyses on time before that; Jim's remarks in April; no complaints before that*
>
> HOW MUCH?
>
> *Analyses were one working day late each time; only one instance of rudeness reported*
>
> GETTING WORSE?
>
> *No better last month - she is looking pretty miserable!*

3.3 How easy have you found it to answer the questions? Do you need to check any of the evidence? If so write down what information you still need and how you intend to get hold of it:

> *Has anyone else noticed the rudeness. What does Jane think? How was she on the phone 3 months ago? How does she get on with Jim?*

3.4 As a result of answering the questions, try to redefine the problem as it is now emerging:

> *In the last two months Margaret has been late with the analyses for my report but not with anything else; Jim alone thinks she is rude*

Once a problem has been fully clarified, a solution will often become apparent. Once the confusion and emotion of a worrying issue has been cleared away by *analysis*, the action to put things right soon gains its proper perspective.

4. Taking action

It is the essence of problem-solving that people would rather come up with *solutions* than clarify what is actually going wrong. We all like suggesting solutions, we all have hunches as to what is happening and what should be done about it.

These must be resisted until the analysis process is complete, because the first solution will often turn out to be inappropriate to the *real* issue that eventually emerges.

As soon as you have a proper focus on the *real* issue you can identify the possible causes of the problem as now defined. There may be one or a number of causes, but each should be checked against the evidence you have collected.

With problems related to people it is rare for there to be one cause; people's behaviour is usually due to a number of factors. As a result there will probably be a number of courses of action you can take to remove those causes.

When clear courses of action become apparent through analysis, they can become the basis of a plan to solve the problem, and as such should be written down as *target statements*. What is to be done, and by whom? How will we know when the target has been achieved? (See Volume 1, *Managing Operations*.)

4. Taking action

How clear are you about the action you should now take to resolve the problem?

4.1 In the light of the evidence you now have, list down the most likely cause(s) of the problem as now defined:

> *Jim changed procedure for monthly analysis reporting last March without consulting Margaret; she thinks he's trying to take her work away. I was annoyed because my report was late again and the rudeness report reinforced my 'negative Pygmalion' attitude.*

4.2 List down actions which would overcome the likely causes of the problem: Who will do what by when?

> *Jane will arrange a meeting by 4 May with Margaret for me to clarify importance of analyses to my report and find out impact of changes since March. I will find out how she gets on with Jim. I will remind Jim of importance of consultation and of Margaret's experience, and clarify roles and priorities with both of them together by 12 May.*

It is also as well to check that the action you now want taken to put the problem right is in line with your own or other people's roles. Does the action fit the structure, and how does the new task link to tasks already agreed and underway? (See 'Clarifying Roles' in Volume 1, *Managing Operations*.)

The final step is to check back to make sure that the targets once achieved will effectively remove the problem as clarified. Clearly the better defined the problem statement the easier it will be to make this judgement.

But if the problem statement suggests the problem is still too large and unmanageable either for adequate definition or for specific actions to be identified, move to the 'Focusing' process to help you break the problem down into smaller units (see Focusing on the Key Issues in Volume 3, *Managing Information*). The smaller you make the problem the easier it will be to take appropriate action, and 'Focusing' will enable you to do that in a positive and creative manner.

There is a tendency when monitoring to look for the things that are not up to standard, the things that are going wrong, the 'problems'. But we must remember that monitoring *progress* suggests things getting better, results improving.

It is therefore important to identify when performance *exceeds* the standards agreed, when a special effort has been made and success achieved. The boss who only criticizes poor performance and never remarks on excellent results is unlikely to provide leadership or motivate effectively.

Acknowledging success and developing the talent that achieves results not only makes the most of resources in the short term, but also ensures that long-term capabilities become available for potential challenges ahead.

4.3 *Check your proposed action against the statement of the problem in Section 3.4. Are you confident that as a result of this action the problem will now be removed?*

Both are conscientious - counselling both separately and then together should resolve the issue

4.4 *Write down an occasion when targets were actually exceeded:*

Jim got budget sheets together without hassle three days early

How did you obtain the information?

He made sure I knew when they were in, and Jane commented

4.5 *How did you act upon this information?*

I just thanked him without any comment. I was concerned about the problem with Margaret at the time

How else could you have made more of this evidence of achievement?

Special acknowledgement would have made seeing him about Margaret easier, and reinforced his ability to work well with peers

PROBLEM WORKSHEET

Write a first draft statement of a problem you have. Identify the relevant target and evidence of the actual situation, and, as a result, re-define your original statement. List the possible cause(s) of *this* problem and the action you intend to take to resolve it.

STATEMENT OF THE PROBLEM:

Our most experienced clerk has been here too long – she's no longer interested in the job.

TARGET:

Margaret should complete all analyses by the last Friday of each month and handle all queries without complaint.

EVIDENCE OF THE ACTUAL SITUATION

WHAT? *Analyses for March and April were not ready for my last two-monthly reports; other information was on time. Jim has remarked on her rudeness on the phone, but no evidence from anyone else*

WHO? *Margaret's analyses, no-one else's information was late.*

WHERE? *Rude on phone to other section members of our department, but not to people outside our department.*

WHEN? *Late end of March and April. Rudeness on only one occasion in April*

HOW MUCH? *One day late each month. No other complaints or relationships affected. Her other work is O.K.*

GETTING WORSE? *Trend of two months. She looks pretty miserable these days!*

REDEFINED STATEMENT OF PROBLEM:

In the last two months Margaret has been late with the analyses for my report but not with anything else; only Jim has reported her rudeness to other Section members.

POSSIBLE CAUSES OF THE PROBLEM:

Jim changed procedure for monthly analysis reporting last March without consulting Margaret. She's told Jane she's sure he's trying to take work away from her – 'Jim always knows best'.

I was annoyed because my report was late again and Jim's 'rudeness' report reinforced my 'negative Pygmalion' attitude towards her. Jane also tells me Margaret's husband lost his job in March...

ACTIONS TO RESOLVE:

Jane will arrange a meeting by 4 May with Margaret for me to clarify importance of analyses to my report and find out impact of changes since March. Check how she gets on with Jim – are there any other problems? How is her husband now? I will remind Jim of importance of consultation before change and the value of Margaret's experience. I will clarify roles and priorities with both of them at a meeting no later than 12 May.

PROBLEM WORKSHEET

Write a first draft statement of a problem you have. Identify the relevant target and evidence of the actual situation, and, as a result, re-define your original statement.   List the possible cause(s) of *this* problem and the action you intend to take to resolve it.

STATEMENT OF THE PROBLEM:

TARGET:

EVIDENCE OF THE ACTUAL SITUATION

WHAT?

WHO?

WHERE?

WHEN?

HOW MUCH?

GETTING WORSE?

REDEFINED STATEMENT OF PROBLEM:

POSSIBLE CAUSES OF THE PROBLEM:

ACTIONS TO RESOLVE:

Monitoring Progress
links to other skills in
the Manager's Toolkit series

Monitoring Progress links to the majority of other skills from the toolkit on page 13 (1, 2, 3, 4, 6, 11 and 12).

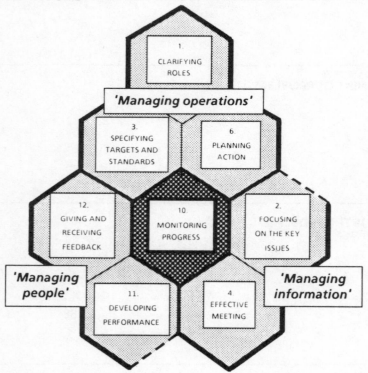

The 'Operations' skills (1, 3, and 6) provide the performance base for monitoring individuals and groups. Focusing (2) breaks problems down into smaller units for action, while meetings (6) remain an essential source of monitoring information.

Developing individuals (11) and providing them with feedback (12) can only be carried out effectively with adequate methods of monitoring in place.

Index

bold type denotes main references